SHED HEAVEN

SHED HEAVEN

ANNA GROVES

National Trust

For Tony 'Three-Shed' Groves,
my really quite erudite father.

First published in the United Kingdom in 2021 by
National Trust Books
43 Great Ormond Street
London
WC1N 3HZ

An imprint of Pavilion Books Ltd.

Volume © National Trust Books, 2021
Text © Anna Groves, 2021

ISBN 978-1-91165-701-9

A CIP catalogue record for this book is available from the
British Library.

10 9 8 7 6 5 4 3 2 1

Reproduction by Rival Colour Ltd, UK
Printed and bound by Toppan Leefung Ltd, China

This book is available at National Trust shops and online
at www.nationaltrustbooks.co.uk, or try the publisher
(www.pavilionbooks.com) or your local bookshop.

TITLE PAGE The Shack, Mottistone Gardens, Isle of Wight.

OPPOSITE Dylan Thomas's Writing Shed, Laugharne, Carmarthenshire.

CONTENTS

INTRODUCTION

The shed, in essence, or at least in the dictionary, is a structure, often open-fronted, for storing or shelter (*Chambers English Dictionary*). The gardener has certainly made the shed his or her own, using it for the safe-keeping of tools, copious flowerpots and bundles of bailing twine. Exactly what the gardener keeps in their shed depends on their own horticultural skills, ambitions and preferences, making the shed as individual as its owner. However, whilst the shed has been commandeered as the horticulturalist's HQ, it's not limited to gardens, as you'll see in the first chapter (A Place for Everything).

A dip into the dictionary also reveals that the word is a variant of 'shade', derived from the old Anglo-Saxon *scead*, making it a quiet place away from the hustle and bustle of life, a sort of hermitage. Many a shed-owner would relate to that, removing themselves to the bottom of the garden for an hour or two of 'pottering', that essential shed-based activity.

Pottering is less easy to define, covering as it does a limitless variety of activities, as long as they're pursued without any sense of urgency and often without any obvious purpose – a form of mindfulness practised in many a shed long before the concept became popular. There are those that potter on a higher plane and in a few sheds, as you'll see in chapter two (A Creative Space), some of those luminaries have used the peace and quiet they've found in their sheds to create timeless works of art.

In part it's the environment inside the shed that's conducive to creativity, but it's also what's outside the shed. Surrounded on all sides by greenery and the sounds and the colours of the natural world, sheds keep you outside and closer to nature whilst keeping you dry. Some sheds have travelled beyond the confines of the back garden and a selection of little sheds in the great outdoors can be found in chapter three (The Inside Out). The focus being on the views or on the nature that the shed gives

OPPOSITE Sauna shed, Carmarthenshire.

immediate access to, these are not sheds for show, but these get a chapter of their own.

The final chapter (Just for Fun) is for the sheds with something to shout about. Many will be familiar with the 'Shed of the Year' competition, which has been running since 2007. However, show sheds, the summer houses of the landed gentry, have been around for a while. The wonderful thing is that now you don't need an estate of many acres to build a folly in the form of a shed. Companies manufacture all manner of glamorous garden buildings nowadays, from pods to geodesic domes, with shades of sage green being particularly popular. These cover a hugely varying range of budgets, but it may be that some of the sheds illustrated in this book will inspire you to get a bit creative customising your own. Happy pottering!

OPPOSITE Shed near Bamburgh Castle, Northumberland.

And everything in its place. At the risk of stating the obvious, most sheds are found in gardens and mostly they're used for storing the stuff of gardening. However, sheds are not limited to the stockpiling of gardening essentials; for centuries the alternative to cultivating the land has been to harvest the seas, so sheds have long been fishermen's friends too. And any occupation or hobby with enough gear to fill a workshop can find a home from home, a few yards away from home, at the bottom of the garden.

GARDENER'S SHED

HIDCOTE, GLOUCESTERSHIRE

Hidcote's garden is world-famous and one of the
National Trust's most-visited gardens. It was highly
regarded and widely celebrated when it was created in
the 1930s by American anglophile Lawrence Johnston.
Today, it is considered to be one of the most important
Arts and Crafts-inspired gardens in the country.

Little wonder, then, that such a garden takes an
arsenal of hoes and rakes, spades and shears, scissors and
dibbers, saws and more to keep it in trim. At 10 acres it is
not the National Trust's largest garden – far from it – but
its design of partitioned but interlinked 'rooms' makes
considerable work for the dozen or so full-time gardeners
and small army of volunteers. But there's no harm in
that, as one of the central tenets of the Arts and Crafts
movement is the celebration of manual labour and the
crafting of natural materials. In place of walls, Hidcote's
garden rooms use box hedging, interwoven branches

of hornbeam and topiary, and in place of doorways are pillars and pergolas strategically placed for the most arresting views.

Starting in 1907 with what was effectively a blank canvas – his mother Gertrude Winthrop bought a farmhouse with lawns and a kitchen garden – Johnston created the Circle, the Fuchsia Garden, the Bathing Pool Garden and the Red Borders with twin gazebos. Johnston downed his gardening tools to fight in the First World War, resuming work in 1919 and adding the Long Walk, the Wilderness, Mrs Winthrop's Garden, the Pillar Garden and the Rock Bank. In the 1920s Johnston then set about collecting foliage from all over the world for his garden, and now logged in the National Trust's database are over 4,000 live plants. The care of all this is a year-round occupation, the four and a half miles of hedges taking eight of those 12 months to trim.

If you go to Hidcote, you'll stand in rapt attention before the 22 beautifully clipped sentinels of the Pillar Garden; you'll gaze at the reflected topiary birds in the Bathing Pool; and you'll perhaps bask in the mid-summer fiery glow of the Red Borders. But hopefully you'll also take a moment to appreciate the gardener's shed – for what would an Arts and Crafts-inspired garden be without its workers and their tools?

HERB GARDEN SHED

SMALLHYTHE PLACE, KENT

It's hard to imagine a prettier looking shed with its steep tiled roof and shuttered window, the little garden before it quartered into neat beds containing medicinal and culinary herbs. This miniature house with path leading up to its front door sits in its miniature plot in the gardens at Smallhythe Place, the former home of actress Ellen Terry. As well as a herb garden, Smallhythe has an orchard, a nuttery and a wildflower bed. Ellen Terry was fondest of roses, which grow in great abundance here – there are over 60 varieties in the rose garden, now including *Rosa* 'Ellen Terry'.

THE DAFFODIL-PACKING SHED

COTEHELE, CORNWALL

Gardening on a *much* larger scale here. Market gardening was once a major industry in the Tamar Valley, which up until the 1950s employed more than 3,000 people. Come spring, that number would swell to 10,000. Along with apples, cherries and strawberries, daffodils were grown in glorious, nodding abundance. A favourable climate and fertile earth – sometimes enriched with 'dock dung' (sweepings from the streets of Plymouth) – ensured teams of daffodil pickers were kept busy through the spring. Once picked, the flowers were taken to packing sheds, like this one at Cotehele.

The steep sides of the Tamar Valley refused to cooperate with machinery and unable to keep up with foreign competition, the industry has all but died out. Daffodils may no longer be a mainstay of the local economy, but they are still much cherished in the Tamar Valley and Cotehele, which grows around 120 varieties and celebrates this favourite herald of spring with a two-week-long festival each year.

FENMAN'S WORKSHOP

WICKEN FEN NATURE RESERVE, CAMBRIDGESHIRE

The National Trust has been looking after Wicken Fen since 1899, just four years after the organisation was founded, making it the Trust's oldest nature reserve. This area of fenland escaped being drained and turned over to farming in the Middle Ages, but continued to have its uses for centuries.

Fenmen made their livings here, digging up peat and harvesting reeds and sedge, which is the grass-like plant that grows in such abundance in these marshy parts. Reed is well known as traditional roofing material and sedge too was used for thatch, but also for fencing, rope-making and basket-weaving. Another harvest was alder buckthorn, as charcoal made from this shrub was used in the manufacture of gunpowder. Fenmen also included working with willow in their repertoire, as well as hunting in the wetlands for eel, ducks and geese.

Some of these traditional occupations can be seen in this recreation of a 1930s fenman's workshop. The wooden decoys are a dead giveaway for the ducks this fenman used to hunt, and there are bodkins galore for basket-weaving. This workshop also boasted a pole lathe, a wood-turning lathe with origins so old they can only be guessed at; a Viking example was found near York. This tool uses the natural springiness found in freshly felled and unseasoned timber and converts it into a rotating motion for turning wood.

This was clearly the workshop of a bodger – not the maligned and misunderstood DIY enthusiast the term has come to denote, but a highly skilled wood-turner. A bodger was often itinerant, so the work could be done close to where the wood was felled. They may have only done the legs for tables, chairs and stools, which they sold on to another craftsman for assembly, but their part they did with skill and specialist equipment. Something to remember the next time you're accused!

BOAT SHEDS

LINDISFARNE CASTLE, HOLY ISLAND, NORTHUMBERLAND

While they may look like a new take on seaside glamping, a holiday haven for hipsters, these sheds are entirely traditional to Holy Island and the practice of its fishermen of repurposing old boats as storage sheds. Thinking that it was a sin to scrap their boats – living on Holy Island you'd expect them to be especially sensitive to sin – the fishers of this island upturned their old herring boats, made a few modifications, added some doors and made themselves perfect little storage sheds for their nets, tools and other equipment. This early form of recycling was practised all along the coast of North East England, but only on Holy Island have they survived in such numbers. The reason these boat sheds at Lindisfarne Castle are in such good condition is that they had to be replaced following a fire in 2005 that badly damaged the originals.

FISHERMAN'S SHED

VOE, OLNA FIRTH, SHETLAND ISLANDS

If the fishermen of Holy Island were resourceful types who carefully conserved what they had, consider this beautifully minimalist scene. It could be titled *Zen and the Art of Fly Fishing*.

This shed floats a little way offshore from the village of Voe in the Shetland Islands, Britain's most northerly group of islands whose waters – which include over 300 lochs – are some of Europe's richest fishing grounds. This loch, Olna Firth, had a thriving herring industry in the 1800s, a whaling station for a regrettable two

decades in the early 1900s, and in the 1950s and 1960s attracted anglers from mainland Britain and beyond for its sea trout.

Olna Firth is connected to the sea, but Voe is actually about as far from the open sea as it is possible to get in Shetland. If the Shetland Islands can be said to have a central point, this is it, but so connected to the sea are these islands that you're never far from the water's edge – about two feet for the owner of this shed!

NET SHOPS

HASTINGS, EAST SUSSEX

Taking the humble shed to new heights are these net shops, found on Hastings seafront. Most of the 50 tall black wooden sheds were built in 1834 for the storage of nets and are still in use today, the tarring of their weatherboards explaining both their stark colour and excellent preservation.

The shingle beach by which the net shops cluster is known as the Stade, taking its name from the Anglo-Saxon word for 'landing place'. Fishing here has a history of a thousand years and counting, as it's still an important activity in the town, even if its importance is more in heritage than economic terms. The Stade is home to Europe's largest fleet of beach-launched fishing boats. Because the boats have to be hauled up the beach after each fishing trip, they are all relatively small – under 33 feet – and that limits how much they can carry and how far they can travel. It also means this fleet fishes in an extremely ecologically considerate and sustainable way, and in possibly much the same way that fishermen have been landing their catches in this area for the last 1,000 years.

What has changed a great deal over the last 200 years is the size of the beach. When the net shops were built, it was very much smaller, hence one fisherman's very bright idea of building upwards to get the most storage in a small space. But then towards the end of the 19th century, a groyne was constructed, stopping the drift of shingle along the coast and so the beach grew. Though this is a working fishery and no museum, visitors are welcome on the Stade and many of the net shops sell fish fresh off the boats.

GARDENER'S SHED

LAMB HOUSE, RYE, EAST SUSSEX

Back in the familiar environs of the back garden, we come now to Rye, where the author Henry James (1843–1916) once lived and wrote. He gained fame for novels such as *The Portrait of a Lady* and *The Turn of the Screw*, which featured both English and American characters, and James lived both sides of the Atlantic. Born in New York City, he lived in Paris and London before moving to East Sussex in his fifties and putting down considerable roots in Rye, living here for nearly 20 years. He loved and was a keen visitor of gardens, but the author was dismissive about his own horticultural abilities: 'I am hopeless about the garden, which I don't know what to do with and shall never, never know – I am densely ignorant.' So James took the advice of his good friend Alfred Parsons, who was an illustrator, landscape painter and garden designer.

Parsons had provided the illustrations for *The Wild Garden* by William Robinson, in which Robinson was advocating a movement away from Victorian formality to more natural plantings, combining edibles with ornamentals. When Parsons began designing gardens, he too favoured the English cottage garden approach, employing traditional materials, dense plantings and mixed herbaceous borders of hardy perennials, some to

eat, some to look at. Essentially the aim was charm over grandeur, and at Lamb House we can see hints of his influence everywhere.

This overall effect of relaxed informality, however, takes some work, hence the need for a well-stocked shed, tucked away in a corner of the vegetable garden. Not that James, given his self-confessed ignorance of horticulture, would have spent a great deal of time here, preferring to employ a gardener and confine his work to the Garden Room with its inspiring views, views that similarly inspired writer E. F. Benson who lived here after James. This detached building was no shed (it was originally used as a banqueting room) but conveniently leads us on to our next chapter – sheds that cultivated creativity.

Some of the world's greatest minds have done their finest pondering in the humblest lodges: Mark Twain had his Octagonal Gazebo, in which he wrote major portions of *The Adventures of Tom Sawyer*, *Adventures of Huckleberry Finn* and more; fellow American and playwright Arthur Miller wrote *Death of a Salesman* in his shed. And, as the following examples show, our own home-grown creative geniuses have found wellsprings of inspiration at the bottom of the garden.

PAGES 38–39 AND OPPOSITE George Bernard Shaw's writing shed, Ayot St Lawrence, Hertfordshire.

GEORGE BERNARD SHAW'S ROTATING WRITING SHED

SHAW'S CORNER, AYOT ST LAWRENCE, HERTFORDSHIRE

George Bernard Shaw (1856–1950) was a prolific writer, penning more than 60 plays and five novels, and a complex character, who frequently courted controversy with his views and vociferously campaigned on a socialist agenda for much of his life.

Not for him, then, an ivory tower from which to dispense his views on society, politics and religion. No, in a secluded part of the beautiful two-acre garden at Shaw's Corner in the tiny Hertfordshire village of Ayot St Lawrence, where he lived with his wife Charlotte for over 40 years from 1906, is a Shavian shed of a most cunning design.

So cunning, in fact, it featured in the August 1929 edition of US Magazine *Modern Mechanics*: 'A revolving turntable is one of the factors in the splendid health of George Bernard Shaw, famous English author. At the age of 72, he is in the prime of physical condition and attributes it partially to his appreciation of sunlight. Mr. Shaw has a plan to keep the sun shining on him constantly while he works. He has constructed a small hut on his grounds that is built on a turntable. When the morning sun shifts, he merely places his shoulder against the side of the hut and gives it a push so that the warming beams fall through his window at the correct angle.'

Shaw's shed also included an electric heater, a typewriter of course, a bunk for naps in between scenes and a telephone to the house for summoning provisions, so he could quite happily sequester himself for hours without disruption. In fact to ensure his creative isolationism was not broken without very good reason, he gave his writing shed a name – 'London' – so that unwanted visitors could be told he was 'visiting the capital'.

PAGE 45 Shaw stepping out of 'London' in 1946.

VIRGINIA WOOLF'S WRITING LODGE

MONK'S HOUSE, RODMELL, EAST SUSSEX

Contemporary with George Bernard Shaw and as influential on later writers was Virginia Woolf (1882–1941), who, like Shaw, was an advocate of the horticultural hideaway. Though born into the affluent, urbane society of South Kensington, Virginia was a lover of nature, and the time she spent during her childhood in St Ives, Cornwall, had a lasting influence upon her. However, she was destined to make her name in London, in Bloomsbury, where the members of the group that she helped found 'lived in squares, painted in circles and loved in triangles' (a most beautiful quip that is most commonly attributed to the American writer Dorothy Parker, although this is disputed by some).

Virginia lived a far from conventional life but she did marry and she did move to the country with her husband and editor. (Not the love triangle you might expect – Leonard Woolf was both!) In 1919 Leonard and Virginia bought Monk's House in the village of Rodmell, East Sussex. It had no water, no electricity but it came with an orchard, an acre of garden and had a view across the River Ouse towards the South Downs. After 1940, when their London home was bombed, the Woolfs made Monk's House their permanent home.

When Leonard and Virginia moved to Monk's House, she first had a tool shed converted into a space in which she could write; her writing lodge would come later. In that shed Virginia penned many of her best-known works, including *Mrs Dalloway* (1925), *To The Lighthouse* (1927) and *Orlando* (1928). It seems Virginia required a room apart, free from distraction, in which to create. In perhaps her most famous work, *A Room of One's Own* (1929), she asserted that in order for a woman to write fiction she must have two things: a room of her own (with key and lock) and enough money to support herself.

While Virginia locked herself away in her shed every morning – in the afternoons she would take a walk around the village, reportedly with lips moving but not uttering a sound as she tried out her sentences – Leonard busied himself in the garden. Ably assisted by his gardener Percy Bartholomew from 1928, he created a beautiful English country garden of rambling roses, lily ponds and ornamental beds crammed with blooms. After many productive years in the tool shed Virginia decided in 1934 to relocate to this writing lodge for a better view of Mount Caburn and perhaps the more to enjoy Leonard's garden that envelops it.

All this sounds rather idyllic but, according to some, Virginia's working environment bordered on the sordid. Her friend Lytton Strachey, fellow author and founding member of the Bloomsbury Group, described her desk in her London home as being littered with 'filth packets', discarded pen nibs, cigarette ends and scraps of writing. As bucolic as the scene must have been outside her Monk's House writing lodge, inside would have been chaotic. Now looked after by the National Trust, the lodge might not preserve quite the same degree of clutter but still has the views that so inspired her.

BARBARA HEPWORTH'S SUMMER SLEEPING SHED

ST IVES, CORNWALL

Virginia Woolf wrote about St Ives: 'I could fill pages remembering one thing after another that made the summer at St Ives the best beginning to a life conceivable'. Certainly the quality of the scenery and the ever-changing moods of sea and sky have made St Ives a source of inspiration for scores of artists.

One such was abstract artist and sculptor Barbara Hepworth (1903–75). Like Virginia Woolf, Barbara Hepworth was a modernist, who rejected the traditional forms of art, architecture, literature, faith and philosophy. Like Woolf, she was a woman who achieved pre-eminence in a male-dominated field. And like Woolf, she liked a nap in her shed.

In what is now the Barbara Hepworth Museum and Sculpture Garden, you'll find her summer sleeping shed tucked into luxuriant foliage in a plot that is small but tropical in the way that many Cornish gardens manage to be. Little wonder this pervading sense of calm – and regular naps – helped to create those amazing curvilinear forms that were a trademark of Barbara Hepworth's work.

PAGE 53 (RIGHT) Hepworth in her garden, 1963.

REVEREND HAWKER'S POETRY HUT

MORWENSTOW, CORNWALL

Staying in Cornwall, we go now to Morwenstow, where the eccentric Reverend Robert Stephen Hawker (1803–75) might have been expected to tend his flock, but spent rather more time smoking opium, writing poetry and salvaging the bodies of shipwrecked sailors from the sea. He was an animal lover, had a pet stag called Robin and went for walks with a pig named Gyp. Oh, and he did all this dressed in a claret-coloured coat, blue fisherman's jersey, fisherman's boots, a brimless pink hat and a poncho made from a yellow horse blanket. For this he certainly gained a reputation locally, but he was name-checked by none other than Charles Dickens, who credited him as the author of the famous Cornish anthem 'The Song of the Western Men' in his magazine *Household Words*.

While he was certainly far from the typical Victorian curate, there is no doubting Reverend Hawker's compassion for his fellow man. Before he came to Morwenstow, sailors who had gone down with their ships were either buried on the beach where they were washed up or left in the sea. Finding this unacceptable, Reverend Hawker built his hut out of driftwood on cliffs overlooking the Atlantic. There he would write his poetry while keeping an eye out for shipwrecks. It's believed he recovered nearly 50 bodies in order to give them a Christian burial. Hawker's Hut is now the National Trust's smallest property but it has a far bigger story than you could ever imagine just by looking at it.

DYLAN THOMAS'S WRITING SHED

Again, perched high on a cliff, a poet finds in a simple outhouse the freedom from distraction to compose his lines. This poet was Dylan Thomas (1914–53), who converted a garage into his writing shed at the Boathouse in Laugharne, where he lived with his wife Caitlin for the last four years of his life. Here it's thought he wrote part of his most famous work, *Under Milk Wood*, and the poem 'Over Sir John's Hill' immortalised the view Thomas enjoyed from his writing shed over the Tâf Estuary to the hills beyond.

Today the Boathouse and Thomas's writing shed are run as a museum by Carmarthenshire County Council. They have been restored to their 1950s appearance, with a degree of the clutter that would have surrounded Thomas as he wrote, as well as the pictures of his heroes – Byron, Walt Whitman, W. H. Auden – that he had tacked up around his desk.

When the light wasn't flooding in through the large window overlooking the estuary, oil lamps provided illumination. When temperatures tumbled, there was a coal-fired stove to stave off the cold; but in the summer months, as Thomas wrote to a friend, 'My study, atelier, or bard's bothy, roasts on a cliff-top.' This description suggests Thomas bent himself in earnest to his writing when in his shed, with just a supply of boiled sweets to keep energy levels topped up. If he wanted sustenance in liquid form, there was Brown's Hotel in Laugharne, but Caitlin was known to lock her husband in his shed to keep the bard from the bar.

ROALD DAHL'S WRITING HUT

GREAT MISSENDEN, BUCKINGHAMSHIRE

Fellow Welshman and occasional poet, but far better known as one of the 20th century's greatest storytellers for children, Roald Dahl (1916–90) created a large and much-loved body of work. He wrote 17 children's novels, three collections of children's verse, as well as adult fiction and non-fiction and many short stories. A 30-year marriage to American actress Patricia Neal produced five children, so he had an audience on whom he could try out his new material, but finding the space and peace in which to write in such a busy household was a trickier matter.

Roald Dahl has been a favourite of millions of children worldwide, but one of his favourite authors was none other than Dylan Thomas. In fact, it was after a pilgrimage to Dylan Thomas's writing shed in the 1950s that Roald Dahl was inspired to create his own, closely modelled on what he'd seen at Laugharne. So in the garden of the family home Roald Dahl gave the

task of recreating Thomas's writing shed to local builder and friend, Wally Saunders. (Some say Wally was the inspiration for the BFG; others say it was more of a self-portrait, as both were very tall, large-eared men.)

Like Dylan Thomas, Roald Dahl pinned photos up on the walls, kept mementoes on his desk – including a ball made from the silver wrappings of chocolate bars and his own hipbone! – and had a supply of boiled sweets close at hand. The main difference between the two authors' writing sheds was that Roald Dahl preferred to shut the light out and work under an angle-poise lamp.

Like Virginia Woolf, Dahl kept to a regular writing schedule: two hours in the morning, a break for lunch and then two more hours in the afternoon. Like George Bernard Shaw, Roald Dahl had a telephone installed and like Shaw, Dahl made up lines to keep unwanted visitors at bay. Dahl didn't tell his children he'd gone to London, however; he told them they'd be eaten by wolves!

Roald Dahl was evidently very pleased with his bolthole. On BBC Radio 4's *Desert Island Discs* in 1979, he described it as: 'A little hut, curtains drawn so I don't see the squirrels up in the apple trees in the orchard. The light on, right away from the house, no vacuum cleaners, nothing… When I am in this place it is my little nest. My womb.'

OPPOSITE Dahl at work in his writing hut, 1965.

THOMAS HARDY'S EARTH CLOSET

HIGHER BOCKHAMPTON, DORSET

This is a writer's hut of a very different nature; in fact, one that relates to the call of nature. As a writer capable of capturing the natural world at its most transcendent and sublime, from *Tess Of The D'urbervilles* to *The Woodlanders*, Thomas Hardy (1840–1928) has few rivals. So it's hoped that fans of Hardy's work won't be offended by the association of his creative genius with something as functional as an earth closet.

The cottage that Thomas Hardy was born in is picture-postcard perfection: its thatch making eyebrows over the windows; woodland to inspire young writers; winding paths through a country garden of roses, foxgloves, hollyhocks and honeysuckle. Also typical of rural living in 19th-century Dorset is the outdoor toilet tucked away in a corner of the garden shed. If you had the means that is – Thomas Hardy's father was a stonemason with employees, so the family was not poor by local standards – and Dorset at that time wasn't all bucolic simplicity,

a particular problem being the disposal of sewage. In Fordington, just over two miles away, there were two deadly outbreaks of cholera, in 1849 and 1854. However, this story, unlike many of Hardy's, has a happy ending.

Father of Thomas Hardy's childhood friend Horace and the vicar of Fordington, the Reverend Henry Moule reacted to his parishioners' suffering by inventing the dry earth closet. He found that when dry earth was mixed with waste, it was fully broken down and odourless in a few weeks, the action of aerobic soil bacteria. He patented his invention – essentially a chamber containing dry earth which was released into a bucket by turning a handle – and for a while it was adopted in private houses in rural districts, military bases and in many hospitals. Thomas Hardy's and Reverend Moule's gifts to humanity were very different, but both undeniably improved the quality of people's lives.

THE SHACK

MOTTISTONE GARDENS, ISLE OF WIGHT

There has been a manor house in the village of Mottistone on the Isle of Wight since the Domesday Book was completed in 1086. It was improved in the Elizabethan era, engulfed by a landslide during the reign of Queen Anne and then bought and restored by Charles Seely, one of the wealthiest industrialists of the Victorian age. But for all Mottistone's history, one of its most eye-catching features is a 1930s garden office called The Shack.

It was designed by architect and great-grandson of Charles Seely, John Seely, and his partner Paul Edward Paget. In 1926 John's father had moved to Mottistone, up until which time the house had been let to tenant farmers and the gardens used as a farmyard. John Seely and Paul Paget had formed their architectural firm in 1922 and were tasked with the remodelling of Mottistone. As part of their renovations Seely and Paget designed The Shack

to double as their drawing office and country retreat. There are two well-lit desks, two comfortable armchairs pulled up to the fire and two bunk beds. Everything is as well considered and laid out as you would expect in an architect-built garden office, with cooker, sink, fridge and even a small en-suite shower room hidden away behind panelling.

John Seely and Paul Paget's partnership was long and successful, the pair almost inseparable over the 40 years they worked together – they referred to each other simply as 'the partner'. In that time they restored such prestigious landmarks as Lambeth Palace, Eton College, Fulham Palace and many London churches – the Second World War had provided much work for architects in the 1950s and 1960s. When John Seely died in 1963, it was his wish that the gardens of Mottistone and The Shack be given to the National Trust for the enjoyment of all.

THE
INSIDE
OUT

These boltholes may be basic and make far less of a statement compared to some, but with these it's not what's on the outside that counts – it's what's outside the outside that makes these sheds so special. We all know the joys of the outdoors, but the experience can suffer somewhat when the wind blows and the heavens open. We've seen sheds for useful storage, sheds for quiet contemplation and now sheds for sheltering from the elements.

PAGES 74-75 Beach huts at Llanbedrog, Gwynedd, Wales.
OPPOSITE Boat shed at Pitlochry, Loch Dunmore, Scotland.

BIRD HIDE

WHITEFORD BURROWS, CWM IVY, GOWER

In terms of sheds not for show, this is very much a case in point. If its four walls of timber interrupted only by a door and a narrow slit of a window make it far from eye-catching, that's a good thing. A bird hide such as this one near Whiteford Burrows National Nature Reserve is designed to be as unobtrusive as possible. Overlooking Cwm Ivy Marsh, it affords birdwatchers the opportunity to observe nature while protecting them from the worst of her elements. Whiteford Burrows at the far end of Gower's north coast is internationally recognised as an important feeding ground for wading birds and wildfowl, including oystercatcher, knot, pintail and golden plover. Here in the marsh, curlews, Europe's largest wading

birds, can be seen probing the waters for worms, shellfish and shrimps with their distinctive down-curved bills. In the spring and summer months, listen for the other-worldly cries of breeding lapwings as they defend their territory. You may even be lucky enough to spot a visiting osprey, Britain's only fish-eating bird of prey. Hen harriers are another ornithological highlight of Cwm Ivy Marsh. This red-listed species is the rarest bird of prey in the UK but they can sometimes be spotted hunting on the marsh in the winter months, a time of year when a hide is handier still.

THE COASTGUARD'S HUT

LLŶN PENINSULA, GWYNEDD

At the end of a narrow winding path, perched high on the top of a headland of the Llŷn Peninsula, you'll find the Cwt Gwylwyr y Glannau Mynydd Mawr (Lookout Hut on the Shores of the Big Mountain). The panoramic views take in the Irish coast to the west, Snowdonia to the east, Anglesey to the north and Bardsey Island to the south. There is beauty all around but danger also in the waters below, so coastguards erected this hut to protect themselves from the elements while they kept lookout for vessels in distress. It was called into military service during the Second World War when fears of invasion were high. They brought reinforcements – up to 70 members of the RAF were stationed here – and built more huts, but today only this and one other survive. The coastguards moved out in 1990 and today the site is looked after by National Trust volunteers and rangers.

BEACH HUTS

The beach hut. Shed *sur mer*. Simplicity itself, its nattily painted façade elevates it above what is simply a shed on a beach and inspires a peculiar nostalgia for the sort of seaside holidays most of us have never actually experienced. While the sight of a row of colourful beach huts can be something quite uplifting they have, of course, a very practical function. The Victorians, newly mobilised by train travel, loved a day trip and took especially to enjoying the seaside and a bracing swim. But the morality of the age made the business of publicly undressing to change into swimsuits problematic. The ever-inventive Victorians came up with the horse-drawn wooden 'bathing-machine' with its protective 'modesty-hood', which would actually be rolled into the water so bathers could make discreet entrances and exits. Beach huts were developed as a more permanent solution to the modesty issue and became a fashionable fixture of many seaside resorts, often converted from bathing machines, fishermen's huts or boat sheds. Fashions naturally wax and wane, and in the early 20th century beach huts were considered holiday homes for the less well-off. However, by the time the British were allowed back on the beaches after the Second World War, beach huts enjoyed what was probably their heyday only then to experience another revival inspired by 1990s tastes for 1950s retro glamour. Such was the demand that it fuelled huge price rises and beach huts in Dorset were being 'snapped up' for six-figure sums! All that has thankfully calmed down now but our fondness for the beach hut remains.

OPPOSITE AND PAGES 86-87 Beach hut, Frinton-on-Sea, Essex.

BEACH HUT

ORFORD NESS, SUFFOLK (2015)

So iconic is the beach hut and redolent of the glory
days of the British seaside that it was chosen as the
visual centrepiece of a travelling art installation.
Commissioned by the National Trust in 2015 to celebrate
the 50th anniversary of Enterprise Neptune, the Trust's
campaign to safeguard the British coastline, 'One and
All' comprised three artworks by sound artist Martyn
Ware (founder of The Human League and Heaven 17),
poet Owen Sheers and visual artist Tania Kovats. The
common theme was the exploration of the powerful
emotional links we all have to coastal landscapes. Ware's
contribution was the creation of a soundscape titled
'What Does the Sea Say?' accompanied by a video, both
of which played in this beach hut as it travelled to three
locations – here at Orford Ness in Suffolk, Ynys Barri in
Pembrokeshire and the Black Beaches, County Durham
– before being displayed at Somerset House, London.
Recordings from the British Library Sound Archive were

played of a range of people talking about their coastal memories, and visitors were invited to record their own experiences and write them up on the walls inside the hut. The visual language of a beach hut and the effect that seascapes have on us are so universally understood that they combined beautifully to form this little museum of memories. It's such a potent bit of imagery, in fact, that a couple of tins of paint is all that would be required to convert your shed into your own candy-striped box of nostalgia.

CAMPING POD

LOW WRAY CAMPSITE, LAKE WINDERMERE, CUMBRIA

If you know someone who says they don't enjoy camping, then they probably haven't tried a camping pod. These locally built wooden pods at the Low Wray Campsite on the western shore of Lake Windermere are so well appointed that some purists might not consider staying in one to be 'real camping'. True, they have lockable French doors; true, they are double-glazed and insulated with sheep's wool to make them both quiet and toasty; and they have a layer of foil in the roof to reflect the summer's heat, so you don't wake up in a suffocating sweat. However, not all of the pods have electricity, so a torch is a required piece of kit, and you'll need it, as inside the pods are beds and little else, so you *will* be making the 3am dash to the toilet block in your pyjamas and hoodie. That and the fact that you step directly out to be greeted by waterfront, lake, meadow or woodland views make these pods the best sort of camping. The only possible down side is that you can't take your canine companion(s) in with you, however dog pods – for one large dog or two small ones – are available.

PITLOCHRY BOAT SHED

LOCH DUNMORE, PERTHSHIRE

You might say Low Wray Campsite, on the shores of Lake Windermere, is on the water. However, it is simply not possible to be *more* on the water than this boat shed on Loch Dunmore in central Scotland. Set in Faskally Wood, its trees precisely reflecting in the still waters of the loch, this shed can only be accessed in one of two ways: by a picturesque timber footbridge and by boat. In autumn, the warm feather-edge cladding blends beautifully with the hues of the trees behind and mirrored in front. Beneath that glassy surface are carp, tench, roach, perch, pike, eels and rudd, making Loch Dunmore a very popular spot with anglers.

JUST FOR FUN

So we've seen that the common-or-garden shed is most often pressed into service for storing gear. And we've also seen the potential of these horticultural hideaways as spaces in which to pursue the cultivation of something more lasting than lettuce. But what if you aren't green-fingered or likely to pen a masterpiece? As the entries for the long-running 'Shed of the Year' competition demonstrate, the shed has become something akin to the follies built by wealthy landowners on their estates. Rather than a place in which to create, these sheds *are* the creation.

PAGES 98-99 Shed of the Year 2015: Inshriach Distillery, Aviemore, Scotland.
OPPOSITE Shed of the Year 2013: Boat shed, Machynlleth, Wales.

SHEDS OF THE YEAR

The shed is a curiously British thing and we know the British are a curious lot. It's been estimated that Britons own around 11.5 million domestic sheds, a higher concentration than can be found anywhere else on the planet. While a great many of those are going to be your common-or-garden six-by-four-foot sheds, there are some that stand out from the crowd, and then there are others that are just dots on the horizon to the crowd.

Since 2007, the title of Shed of the Year has been contested by hundreds of 'shedheads' who can enter their own very personal creations into a variety of categories: Cabin/Summerhouse, Workshop and Studio, Unexpected, Unique, Budget, Nature's Haven and Pub and Entertainment. Overall winners have included a shed cum distillery, a shed cum Roman temple and a shed cum pirate ship poop deck. All are labours of love with considerable time invested, but many demonstrate the sort of frugality that combines so well with imagination.

Take 2013's winning entry, involving a boat dragged up a mountain in Mid Wales and repurposed as a roof. The shed is made from completely recycled materials, including a chimney cut from a pole that used to hold up a circus tent. Set in wattle and daub walls is an assortment of windows from a 1940s caravan and a 400-year-old farmhouse. It's a Womble's paradise, which is a dated reference, but this shed's emphasis on recycling and the reduction of waste makes it entirely relevant.

Another winner that addresses current environmental concerns while being pleasing to look at is 2018's Bee Eco Shed. A giant bughouse has been built against one wall and a spiral staircase leads up to the roof where beehives sit among flowers and vegetables. All this occupies a footprint not much bigger than your average shed. Not everyone has the time and dedication required to be a beekeeper, but pretty much anyone with a shed wall has a vacancy for a bee hotel.

OPPOSITE Shed of the Year 2013: Boat shed, Machynlleth, Wales. PAGE 104 Shed of the Year finalist 2017: Woodland Stargazer, Fort William, Scotland. PAGE 105 Shed of the Year 2018: George Smallwood and his Bee Eco Shed, Sheffield.

THE BOTHY

The Bothy is the creation of designer and maker Will Shannon and stands glorying in its isolation at the top of a steep hill overlooking Standen's garden. As one interested in 'the making of things', Will was naturally drawn to Standen, an Arts and Crafts house built following the principles of that movement, principles that rejected the growing industrialisation of manufacturing in the late-Victorian period and that celebrated craftsmanship and the use of natural and local materials. The pace of mechanisation hasn't exactly slowed in the last 100 years, so it's no wonder that there are still many people like Will who prefer a more artisanal approach.

Will took inspiration from the house at Standen and used a patchwork of materials – brick, tile, timber and stone – all sourced within 10 miles of Standen and assembled by his own highly skilled hands over two weeks in September 2016. The result he titled 'the Bothy' and described it as 'a space to shelter, somewhere for a wanderer to rest, a gardener to shelter in or an artist to draw'. Where a bothy differs from a shed is that a bothy's original function was to provide shelter to walkers in the mountains of Scotland, Northern England, Northern Ireland and Wales. While the climb up to the Bothy hardly calls for crampons, to call it 'the Shed' wouldn't quite convey the same degree of shelter and isolation from the modern world. However, as singular as it is, it is in good company among these sheds of distinction.

THE CHINESE HOUSE

STOWE, BUCKINGHAMSHIRE

Sheds as follies are nothing new. True, if you had an estate and the mind and the money to fill it with follies, you would perhaps tend towards temples, rotundas, bridges and grottoes. However, in some of the finest landscape gardens are more modest buildings that could be regarded – somewhat retrospectively and entirely respectfully – as sheds of the highest order. One such is the Chinese House at Stowe in Buckinghamshire.

Stowe was developed in three main phases with the most noted garden designers and architects at the helm of each. Thought to date from around 1738, the Chinese House is attributed to William Kent, who for 18 years (the middle phase) was the architect of Stowe's landscape and many of its most remarkable buildings. Held against another of Kent's constructions, the Temple of Venus with its busts of Cleopatra, Faustina, Nero and Vespasian, the Chinese House might seem overshadowed. Small it may be but in its original setting – on stilts over water in the middle of a straight-sided pond

(since filled in) – the effect would have been arrestingly beautiful. Though designed to be seen from a distance, the panels on the inside and outside of the Chinese House are filled with intricate scenes, figures of Chinese deities, delicate flowers and careful calligraphy. The same painter who worked on the Temple of Venus was responsible for the Chinese House's decoration, the same care lavished on both.

These Chinese-style pavilions were very much in fashion in the 1730s and were a feature of many designed landscapes. Indeed, this particular Chinese House has graced more than one garden. After a decade or so at Stowe, it was moved to a neighbouring family estate, where it resided for the next 200 years. In the 1950s, when the owner of that estate moved to County Kildare in Ireland, he insisted on taking it with him. It wasn't until the 1990s, after the National Trust's acquisition of Stowe, that the Chinese House was tracked down and brought back to the place for which it was designed.

JAPANESE TEA HOUSE

TATTON PARK, CHESHIRE

The Egerton family owned Tatton Park for nearly 400 years, setting their Neo-classical mansion within 50 acres of landscaped and occasionally highly ornate gardens. The best was undoubtedly saved for the Japanese Garden, created after Alan de Tatton Egerton, 3rd Baron Egerton, visited an Anglo-Japanese exhibition, the first ever, in White City, London in 1910. He didn't just employ the ideas he'd seen at the exhibition, he recruited a team of Japanese workmen, and together they created what is considered by many to be the finest example of a Japanese garden in the UK, if not Europe. Japanese gardens traditionally fall into three categories and it was a tea garden (rather than the more formal hill and dry gardens) that Lord Egerton wanted at Tatton, complete with tea house as its centrepiece. Given his workers' skills and knowledge, the tea house is unsurprisingly no hackneyed pastiche; it was designed with care and authenticity and its placement also considered. It is based on a Japanese mountain hut and, apart from a window at the top to allow light in, the only other window faces east to the rising sun and looks onto the Shinto shrine that Lord Egerton had imported from Japan.

THE SUMMER HOUSE

FLORENCE COURT, COUNTY FERMANAGH

What is a summer house if not a shed built for non-practical, entirely recreational reasons? A little hut of timber built just for fun. That's why we've included summer houses in our selection, and also because hopefully we've demonstrated that sheds aren't limited to being used for the storage of stuff, as places to potter, or rooms to write. You could do all those things in Florence Court's Summer House, but chances are you'd be too captivated by that view to do much besides sit and stare. Beautifully framed in the distance is Benaughlin Mountain, in the foreground the Pleasure Grounds that are a riot of rhododendrons and azaleas in the spring and early summer. Today's Summer House is a reconstruction after the structure that had stood here was consumed by fire in 2014. The original was called the Heather House, after the heather that lined its walls, and was built by the 3rd Earl of Enniskillen in the second half of the 19th century. So the Summer House may be new but such a timeless view demanded a shelter in which to sit and lose hours just looking at it.

PAGE 117 The 3rd Earl of Enniskillen and his family at the original Summer House, c. 1870.

THE BEAR'S HUT

KILLERTON, DEVON

If you go down to Killerton today, you're sure of a big surprise. Indeed the Bear's Hut – though not called that at the time – was built in 1808 as a surprise for Lydia, Lady Acland. Sir Thomas Dyke Acland had been working for some time with his head gardener John Veitch to create a picturesque landscape in the grounds of his country home. Veitch, who was influenced by Lancelot 'Capability' Brown and worked with Brown's successor Humphry Repton, brought to Killerton features made famous by these two great English landscape designers. So you'll find natural-looking clumps of trees scattered across sweeps of gently rolling lawns, sinuous paths guiding you to carefully planned views, and rustic buildings designed to recreate a scene from a pastoral idyll.

Known originally as the 'Lady Cot', this summer house would have played host to many a tea party, and the Aclands certainly made it a very personal space. The interior decoration includes a stained-glass window made of fragments collected by the family, while the walls and ceiling are covered in bark, pine cones and twigs, and the floor of the inner room is somewhat gruesomely 'cobbled' with deer knuckle-bones. Later generations were no less eccentric, as the Lady Cot was renamed the Bear's Hut when a black bear called Tom was brought back from Canada by the 12th baronet's brother, Gilbert, and kept as a pet. Now that *surely* was a surprise!

THE DEN

NELLY'S LABYRINTH, CRAGSIDE, NORTHUMBERLAND

It seems so far that the grown-ups are having all the fun, so here's one just for the kids. If they can make it through Cragside's labyrinth that is. The original labyrinth of Greek mythology was designed by legendary craftsman and inventor Daedalus to hold a monster that was part man, part bull, all terrifying. Minors rather than minotaurs now run riot through this network of winding paths and tunnels cut out of a vast area of rhododendron forest. The comparison might sound fantastical but the man largely responsible for Cragside would probably have enjoyed it. William Armstrong, 1st Baron Armstrong, was a Victorian inventor, technological pioneer and landscape genius. His house was the first in the world to be lit by hydroelectricity and is crammed full of evidence of Lord Armstrong's ingenuity, from the hydraulic lift that took them to bed each night to the extensive central heating system. This octagonal thatched hut sits at the centre of a labyrinth named after a local witch, and why not? For aren't imagination, eccentricity and a willingness to believe in things that others find improbable often found in those who invent?

MINIATURE CARPENTER'S SHOP

NUNNINGTON HALL, NORTH YORKSHIRE

And finally, to emphatically show that sheds come truly in all sizes, here's one in miniature. This tiny carpenter's shop interior was in fact made by a gardener who worked at Pyt House, a small country mansion in south-west Wiltshire. Curious, then, that it should end up in a collection of miniature rooms in Yorkshire. But curious the Carlisle Collection most certainly is. Mrs Carlisle, or Kitty to her close circle, started collecting miniature objects as a child living in India. By the 1930s, married to a successful insurance broker and living in London, her collection had grown so large that she decided to commission skilled craftsmen to build rooms to display her tiny treasures. Over the course of 40 years a variety of settings were created, starting with a Queen Anne Drawing Room and culminating in a Palladian Hall, and included in these models of 17th- and 18th-century aristocratic life is the humble shed. In 1970 Kitty Carlisle gifted her collection of around 10,000 items and 16 rooms to the National Trust, and in 1980 it found its way to Nunnington via Grey's Court in Oxfordshire, where they can still be seen – if you remember to take your glasses!

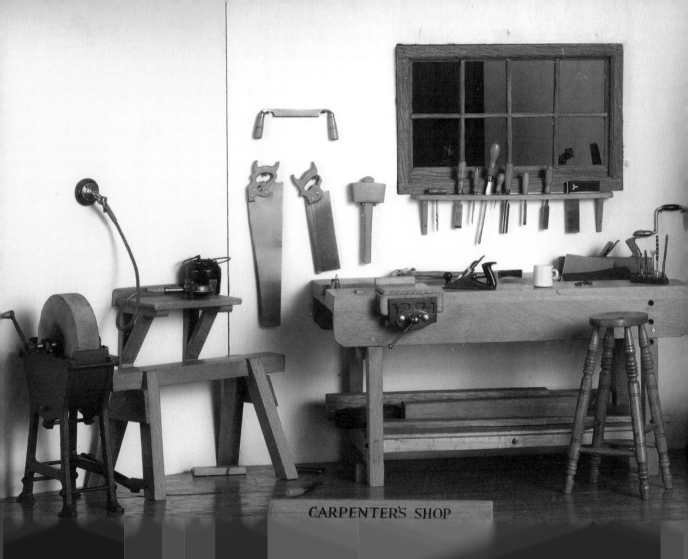

CARPENTER'S SHOP

ABOVE AND OPPOSITE Virginia Woolf's Writing Lodge, Monk's House, Rodmell, Sussex. The photograph above shows (from left to right) Angelica Garnett, Vanessa Bell, Clive Bell, Virginia Woolf, and, partly obscured, John Maynard Keynes and Lydia Lopokova, August 1935.

PICTURE CREDITS

© National Trust Images: NTI/John Miller: 2, 23, 71, 72, 73; NTI/Chris Lacey: 10–11, 35, 55, 56, 67, 68, 69 (both); NTI/Jim Woolf: 13; NTI/Sarah Davis: 15; NTI/Nick Meers: 17, 115; NTI/Arnhel de Serra: 19, 28; NTI/Carole Drake: 21; NTI/Catriona Darroch: 24; NTI/Rob Coleman: 25; NTI/Joe Cornish: 27, 83; NTI/John Millar: 28, 107 (left), 116; NTI/Andrew Butler: 36, 37, 109; NTI/James Dobson: 38–39, 41, 49, 79, 80, 123, 126; NTI/Paul Watson: 44; NTI/Caroline Arber: 47; NTI/Andreas von Einsiedel: 48; NTI/Jo Hatcher: 57; NTI/Justin Minns: 89, 90; NTI/Paul Harris: 93, 94, 95; NTI/Sam Milling: 107 (right); NTI/Stephen Robson: 111; NTI/Tatton Park: 112; NTI/Andy Tryner: 113; NTI/Erne Collection: 117; NTI/Clive Nichols: 119; NTI/Derek Croucher: 121; NTI/Robert Thrift: 125.

Shutterstock: 5, 51, 53 (right), 97, 101, 103, 104, 105. Alamy: 7, 31, 33, 45, 52, 53 (left), 59, 60–61, 63, 74–75, 77, 120, 127. Getty Images: 9, 65. Tina Hillier: 43, 85, 86, 87. © The Gin Cooperative: 98–99.

Front cover (top row, left to right): Boat Sheds, Lindisfarne (©National Trust Images/Joe Cornish), Fenman's Workshop, Wicken Fen (©National Trust Images/John Miller), Japanese Tea House, Tatton Park (©National Trust Images/Stephen Robson); (bottom row, left to right): Gardener's Shed, Hidcote (©National Trust Images/Sarah Davis), Herb Garden Shed, Smallhythe Place (©National Trust Images/Arnhel de Serra), The Shack, Mottistone Gardens (©National Trust Images/John Miller). Back cover: Beach Hut, Orford Ness (©National Trust Images/Justin Minns).